Pink GIN

Pink GIN

more than **30** pink-hued cocktails

RYLAND PETERS & SMALL

LONDON • NEW YORK

Senior Designer Toni Kay
Production Manager
  Mai-ling Collyer
Editorial Director Julia Charles
Art Director Leslie Harrington
Publisher Cindy Richards

Indexer Hilary Bird

First published in 2020 by
Ryland Peters & Small
20–21 Jockey's Fields
London WC1R 4BW
and
341 E 116th Street
New York, 10029
www.rylandpeters.com

10 9 8 7 6 5 4 3 2 1

Original recipe text © Julia Charles,
Laura Gladwin & David T. Smith
Recipe collection and pink gin recipe
adaptations devised by Julia Charles
copyright © Ryland Peters & Small 2020
Design and photographs copyright
© Ryland Peters & Small 2020
See page 64 for full credits.

ISBN: 978-1-78879-214-1

A CIP record for this book is available from
the British Library. US Library of Congress
CIP data has been applied for.

Printed in India

Contents

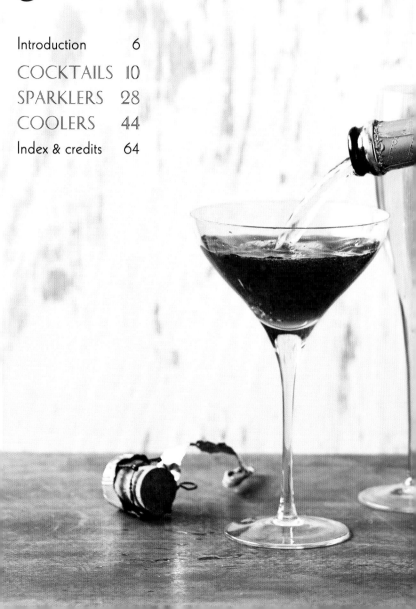

Introduction

Pink gin has never been more popular so why not shake up your own rosy-hued cocktails at home with the perfectly-pink recipes in this book? 'Pink gin' was originally a simple cocktail of London Dry Gin seasoned with a dash of Angostura bitters, but this term has blossomed and is now used to describe bottled gins that have been infused or flavoured with fruits and flowers. These include raspberry, strawberry, rhubarb, pink grapefruit, rose and hibiscus and the resulting blush-coloured spirits, in tones ranging from neon pink to pale pastels, can be enjoyed in a range of delicious drinks. From the simplest G&T to bartenders' favourite the Clover Club, a splash of pink gin will always add a little extra pep to your cocktail drinking experience.

Long-established brands (such as Beefeater) have added berry-bright gins to their ranges, plus sunshine-fuelled Mediterranean distillers, such as Italian Malfy, are all creating elegant citrus-infused pink gins in gorgeous bottles, and all of them make perfect cocktail ingredients. So whether you're a gin expert wanting to update a beloved classic drink, new to the gin scene and keen to try the latest innovations, or have simply found that a fruitier tipple is your thing, you'll find all the pink gin inspiration you need here!

All gins start with a neutral spirit base, which is then infused with juniper and other botanicals, such as spices, citrus, berries and flowers, to give each one a unique taste and its 'style'. A style is usually described as fruity, floral or citrusy. The drinks in the book have been developed using branded gins with particular styles that work well with the other ingredients. In spirit terminology the predominant flavour in a gin is described as being 'flavour-forward', so raspberry-flavour forward and so on. If you can't source the exact gin specified for each recipe, don't worry, simply use the description of its style and key flavour to find something similar to substitute it with and the results will be just as delicious! Some recipes in this book use a flavoured gin liqueur as these are becoming increasingly popular. They are sweeter and more intense than gin and have a lower alcohol content, making them a good choice for long drinks.

Here are a few cocktail-making tips for recipes in this book:

* When crushing (muddling) fruit in the glass or in a cocktail shaker, use a wooden cocktail 'muddler' or the end of a wooden rolling pin.

* Fresh fruit cocktail fruit purées are available to buy online and make a good alternative to fruit for drinks built in a delicate glass or made in large batches.

* Always chill carbonated mixers and sparkling wines well before use so that they are as fizzy as possible.

COCKTAILS

Parisian Martini

THIS SIMPLE BUT DELICIOUS APÉRITIF SHOWCASES TWO OF
FRANCE'S BEST-KNOWN LIQUORS, VERMOUTH AND CASSIS,
AND IS GIVEN A LITTLE *JE NE SAIS QUOI* HERE WITH
A FRUITY RASPBERRY-INFUSED GIN.

35 ml/1$\frac{1}{4}$ fl oz. Pinkster,
or similar raspberry-forward, fruity pink gin
35 ml/1$\frac{1}{4}$ fl oz. dry vermouth
30 ml/1 fl oz. crème de cassis (blackcurrant liqueur)
a lemon zest, to garnish
ice cubes

SERVES 1

Put a martini glass in the fridge to chill.
Fill a cocktail shaker with ice cubes and add the gin,
vermouth and crème de cassis. Stir well and strain
into the chilled glass. Garnish with a lemon
zest and serve immediately.

Pink Martini

THERE ARE PLENTY OF OCCASIONS THAT CALL FOR A FUN,
FLIRTY PINK DRINK, SO HERE IS A CLASSIC, REINVENTED
WITH A DASH OF FRUITY STRAWBERRY GIN.

75 ml/2½ fl oz. Lola & Vera Strawberry Gin,
or similar strawberry-forward, fruity pink gin
10 ml/2 teaspoons dry vermouth
a lemon zest, to garnish
ice cubes

SERVES 1

Put a martini glass in the fridge to chill. Add all the
ingredients to a cocktail shaker filled with ice cubes,
shake sharply and strain into the chilled glass.
Garnish with a lemon zest and serve immediately.

Clover Club

THIS CLASSIC COCKTAIL WAS FIRST RECORDED IN 1917.
IT CONSISTS OF GIN, LEMON JUICE AND RASPBERRY SYRUP
SHAKEN WITH AN EGG WHITE TO GIVE IT A FLUFFY, FOAMY
HEAD. THE ADDITION OF A DASH OF PINK GIN CAN ONLY
ADDS TO ITS ENDURING POPULARITY!

50 ml/1²/₃ fl oz. Warner's Raspberry Gin,
or similar raspberry-forward, fruity pink gin

20 ml/³/₄ fl oz. freshly squeezed lemon juice

5 ml/1 teaspoon raspberry syrup (or Grenadine)

a dash of very fresh egg white

simple sugar syrup, to taste

fresh raspberries, to garnish (optional)

ice cubes

SERVES 1

Add all the ingredients to a cocktail shaker filled
with ice cubes and shake sharply. Strain into
a cocktail coupe, garnish with a few raspberries
(if using) and serve immediately.

Bramble

SIMPLE TO MAKE AND WELL-BALANCED WITH SWEET
AND SOUR NOTES, THE BRAMBLE HAS BECOME SOMETHING
OF A MODERN CLASSIC AND WORKS BEAUTIFULLY
WITH A BLACKBERRY-INFUSED PINK GIN.

50 ml/1²/₃ fl oz. Tarquin's British Blackberry Gin,
or similar blackberry-forward, fruity pink gin
30 ml/1 fl oz. freshly squeezed lemon juice
10 ml/2 teaspoons simple sugar syrup
15 ml/¹/₂ fl oz. crème de mûre (blackberry liqueur)
a lemon wedge and a blackberry, to garnish
ice cubes and crushed ice

SERVES 1

Shake the gin, lemon juice and sugar syrup
in a cocktail shaker with a good handful of ice cubes,
then strain into a rocks glass full of crushed ice. Drizzle
the crème de mûre over the ice and garnish
with a lemon wedge and a fresh blackberry.
Serve immediately.

Pink Lady

THE WHITE LADY IS A SLINKY, SOPHISTICATED 1920S CLASSIC,
BUT ADDING SPARKLING PROSECCO AND CITRUSY PINK GIN
BRINGS THINGS BANG UP TO DATE.

35 ml/1 $\frac{1}{4}$ fl oz. Edgerton Original Pink Gin,
or similar berry-forward, citrusy pink gin

15 ml/ $\frac{1}{2}$ fl oz. Cointreau

15 ml/ $\frac{1}{2}$ fl oz. freshly squeezed lemon juice

well-chilled Prosecco, to top up

ice cubes

SERVES 1

Pour the gin, Cointreau and lemon juice into a cocktail shaker
half-filled with ice cubes. Stir until very cold, then strain into a
martini glass. Top up slowly with Prosecco and serve immediately.

Pinklet

THIS PINK TWIST ON A GIMLET, THE CRISP AND REVIVING APÉRITIF,
IS A SHAMELESS TREAT FOR THE EVER-GROWING NUMBER
OF PINK GIN DEVOTEES OUT THERE.

50 ml/1²/₃ fl oz. Adnams Copper House Pink Gin,
or similar raspberry-forward, fruity pink gin

50 ml/1²/₃ fl oz. Rose's lime cordial

a lime zest, to flavour and garnish

ice cubes

SERVES 1

Put a martini glass in the fridge to chill. Pour the
lime cordial into a cocktail shaker and add a few
ice cubes. Add the gin and stir until the outside of the
shaker feels very cold. Strain into the chilled glass,
garnish with a lime zest and serve immediately.

Marguerite

THIS LESS WELL-KNOWN BUT EXTREMELY SOIGNÉE COUSIN
OF THE MARTINI WOULD BE JUST THE THING TO ORDER
SHOULD YOU EVER FIND YOURSELF WHISKED BACK IN TIME
TO A 1920S PARISIAN BAR. GIVE IT A LITTLE EXTRA
CITRUSY TANG WITH A PINK GRAPEFRUIT GIN.

35 ml/1 1/4 fl oz. Sacred Pink Grapefruit Gin,
or similar grapefruit-forward, citrusy pink gin

30 ml/1 fl oz. dry vermouth

15 ml/1/2 fl oz. triple sec

a dash of Angostura bitters

a twist of orange or pink grapefruit zest, to garnish

ice cubes

SERVES 1

Put a cocktail coupe in the fridge to chill.
Fill a cocktail shaker with ice cubes and
add the gin, vermouth, triple sec and Angostura
bitters. Stir well and strain into the chilled cocktail
coupe. Garnish with a twist of orange or pink
grapefruit zest and serve immediately.

Lucien Gaudin

THIS FRENCH TWIST ON THE ICONIC ITALIAN NEGRONI
FEATURES THE ESSENTIAL CAMPARI, BUT REPLACES THE
SWEET VERMOUTH WITH COINTREAU AND DRY VERMOUTH.
SPLASHING IN A SPANISH ORANGE-INFUSED GIN
ADDS TO ITS CONTINENTAL CHARM...

35 ml/ 1 1/4 fl oz. Tanqueray Flor de Sevilla,
or similar citrus-forward orange gin (or pink) gin
15 ml/ 1/2 fl oz. Campari
15 ml/ 1/2 fl oz. Cointreau
15 ml/ 1/2 fl oz. dry vermouth
an orange zest, to garnish
ice cubes

SERVES 1

Put a martini glass in the fridge to chill. Fill a cocktail
shaker with ice cubes and add the gin, Campari,
Cointreau and vermouth. Stir well and strain into the
chilled glass. Garnish with an orange zest and
serve immediately.

Rosie Lea

IS IT A CLASSY COCKTAIL? A REFRESHING SWEETENED TEA?
OR A FUN DRINK PERFECT FOR AN AFTERNOON TEA PARTY?
YES, YES AND YES.

**120 ml/4 fl oz. Beefeater London Pink,
or similar strawberry-forward, fruity pink gin**

60 ml/2 fl oz. triple sec

320 ml/11 fl oz. cranberry juice

freshly squeezed juice of 1 lime

4 lime slices, to garnish

ice cubes

SERVES 4

Add the gin, triple sec, cranberry and lime juices
to a large clean teapot or a jug/pitcher filled with ice
cubes. Stir well and pour into tea cups or tumblers,
garnish each one with a slice of lime and serve.

Long Pedlar

SLOE GIN IS SWEETENED WITH SWEET, PLUMP
BLACKTHORN BERRIES, WHICH GIVE IT A UNIQUE COLOUR.

50 ml/1^2/$_3$ fl oz. Hayman's Sloe Gin, or similar sloe gin

150 ml/5 fl oz. bitter lemon

lemon zests and bay leaves, to garnish and, if in season,

some fresh sloe berries, ideally embedded in an ice cube

ice cubes

SERVES 1

Fill a large balloon glass with ice cubes. Add the gin and stir until the glass is frosted. Add the bitter lemon, stir again, garnish, and serve immediately.

Sloe Gin Fizz

LIVE LIFE IN THE SLOE LANE WITH THIS REFRESHING LONG
DRINK, A COMBINATION OF JAMMY SLOE GIN AND SODA.

50 ml/1^2/$_3$ fl oz. Sipsmith Sloe Gin, or similar sloe gin

20 ml/^{3}/$_4$ fl oz. freshly squeezed lemon juice

a dash of simple sugar syrup

well-chilled soda water, to top up

a lemon slice, to garnish

ice cubes

SERVES 1

Add all the ingredients, except the soda, to a cocktail shaker filled with ice cubes. Shake and strain into an ice-filled highball glass. Top up with soda water, garnish with a lemon slice and serve immediately.

SPARKLERS

Rosy Glow

TAKING ITS LEAD FROM THE CLASSIC 80S COCKTAIL
SEX ON THE BEACH, THIS FRUITY SPARKLER REPLACES
THE TRADITIONAL PEACH SCHNAPPS AND VODKA
WITH A PEACH-FLAVOURED PINK GIN WITH
DELICIOUS RESULTS.

30 ml/1 fl oz. Buss No.509 Persian Peach Gin,
Kuro Soft Peach Gin, or similar peach-flavoured pink gin

15 ml/$\frac{1}{2}$ fl oz. freshly squeezed orange juice

15 ml/$\frac{1}{2}$ fl oz. cranberry juice

well-chilled Prosecco, to top up

an orange zest or fresh peach slice,
to garnish

ice cubes

SERVES 1

Put a flute in the fridge to chill. Pour the gin, orange juice
and cranberry juice into an ice-filled cocktail shaker and
shake well. Strain into the chilled flute and slowly top
up with Prosecco. Garnish with an orange zest or
a peach slice and serve immediately.

Rosebud

FEISTY YET DELICATE, AND STRANGELY CAPTIVATING... NO, NOT A PLUCKY ROMANTIC HEROINE, BUT A RATHER LOVELY SPARKLING COCKTAIL.

15 ml/$\frac{1}{2}$ fl oz. Bloom Jasmine and Rose Gin, or similar floral pink gin

20 ml/$\frac{3}{4}$ fl oz. St. Germain Elderflower Liqueur

5 ml/1 teaspoon rosewater

5 ml/1 teaspoon freshly squeezed lemon juice

well-chilled Prosecco, to top up

edible rose petals, to garnish (optional)

ice cubes

SERVES 1

Put the gin, St. Germain, rosewater and lemon juice in an ice-filled cocktail shaker. Shake well, strain into a flute and slowly top up with the chilled Prosecco. Garnish with rose petals (if using) and serve immediately.

Raspberry Dazzler

THE THINKING PERSON'S STRAWBERRY IS SHOWN OFF TO BEST ADVANTAGE WITH FRUITY RASPBERRY-INFUSED GIN AND PROSECCO.

25 ml/1 fl oz. Gordon's Premium Pink Gin, or similar raspberry-forward, fruity pink gin

4 fresh raspberries

$\frac{1}{2}$ teaspoon caster/superfine sugar

PopaBall™ Raspberry Bursting Bubbles

well-chilled Prosecco, to top up

ice cubes

SERVES 1

Put the raspberries and sugar in a cocktail shaker and crush with a muddler (or end of a wooden rolling pin). Add the gin and some ice cubes and shake well. Strain into a flute and add a teaspoon of Raspberry Bursting Bubbles. Top up with chilled Prosecco and serve immediately.

Pink Lemonade

THIS TANGY TREAT COMBINES AN ITALIAN
GIN, INFUSED WITH SICILIAN PINK
GRAPEFRUIT, AND LIMONCELLO,
WITH LIP-TINGLING RESULTS.

**30 ml/1 fl oz. Malfy Gin Rosa,
or similar pink grapefruit-forward,
citrusy pink gin**

15 ml/$\frac{1}{2}$ fl oz. limoncello (Italian lemon liqueur)

well-chilled Prosecco, to top up

a strip of lemon zest, to garnish

ice cubes

SERVES 1

Put the gin and limoncello in a cocktail shaker with
a handful of ice cubes and stir until they are very
cold. Strain into a flute and slowly top with chilled
Prosecco. Squeeze the lemon zest in half lengthways
over the drink, so that the essential oils in the skin spritz
over it, then drop it in and serve immediately.

Bridge of Sighs

THIS DRINK WAS NAMED AFTER THE BRIDGE IN VENICE,
UNDER WHICH, LEGEND HAS IT, LOVERS WILL BE GRANTED
ETERNAL BLISS IF THEY KISS ON A GONDOLA AT SUNSET...
IT MIGHT BE EASIER TO JUST DRINK ONE OF THESE!

15 ml/½ fl oz. Old Curiosity Pink Elderflower and Jasmine Gin,
or similar floral pink gin

15 ml/½ fl oz. St. Germain Elderflower Liqueur

well-chilled Prosecco, to top up

caster/superfine white sugar, to rim the glass

ice cubes

SERVES 1

Moisten the rim of a flute with water
and dip it into a saucer filled with sugar to create
a rim around the glass. Set aside. Put the gin and
St. Germain in a cocktail shaker with a handful of ice
cubes and stir. Strain carefully into the sugar-rimmed
flute. Slowly top up with the chilled Prosecco
and serve immediately.

Babycakes

LOOK NO FURTHER FOR THE ULTIMATE VALENTINE'S
SPARKLING COCKTAIL. RED BERRIES, ROSEWATER AND
A FLORAL PINK GIN ARE JUST MEANT TO BE TOGETHER.

60 ml/2 fl oz. Edinburgh Valentine's Gin,
or similar floral pink gin

20 ml/³/₄ fl oz. Chambord

5 ml/1 teaspoon rosewater

well-chilled Asti Spumante or other
semi-sweet sparkling wine, to top up

edible rose petals, to garnish

ice cubes

SERVES 2

Put two flutes in the fridge to chill.
Pour the gin, Chambord and rosewater into an
ice-filled cocktail shaker and stir well. Strain into
the chilled flutes and slowly top up with the
Asti Spumante. Garnish with rose petals
and serve immediately.

Breakfast in Milan

THIS TANGY TIPPLE IS DELICIOUS SERVED WITH A BUTTERY, MELT-IN-THE-MOUTH PASTRY. CONTINENTAL BREAKFAST IN BED, ANYONE?

30 ml/1 fl oz. Slingsby Marmalade Gin,
or similar orange-forward, citrusy orange or pink gin

1 tablespoon shredless orange marmalade/orange preserve

15 ml/¹/₂ fl oz. freshly squeezed lime juice

a dash of Campari (or Aperol for a less bitter taste)

well-chilled Prosecco, to top up

ice cubes

MAKES 1

Put a martini glass in the fridge to chill. Put the
marmalade/preserve in a cocktail shaker with the gin,
lime juice and Campari or Aperol. Half-fill the shaker
with ice cubes and shake vigorously. Strain into
the chilled martini glass and slowly top up
with Prosecco. Serve immediately.

La Rosa Vita

BRING A LITTLE ITALIAN CULTURE TO YOUR NEXT GET-
TOGETHER WITH THIS DELICIOUSLY REFRESHING SPARKLER.
ADDING A LITTLE SPLASH OF PINK GIN, INFUSED WITH
RASPBERRY AND STRAWBERRY, ADDS TO ITS ALLURE.

30 ml/1 fl oz. Echo Falls Summer Berry Pink Gin,
or similar berry-forward, fruity pink gin

30 ml/1 fl oz. raspberry cocktail purée (see page 9)

4 dashes of orange bitters

well-chilled Prosecco or Cava, to top up

SERVES 2

Add the gin, raspberry purée and orange bitters to
a small jug/pitcher and stir to combine. Divide the
mixture between two flutes and slowly top up
with chilled Prosecco or Cava. Stir each one
gently with a long-handled barspoon or
similar and serve immediately.

Blackberry Barfly

DARK AND HEADY, WITH A DELICIOUSLY UNEXPECTED
TANG OF BALSAMIC VINEGAR, THIS SLOE GIN COCKTAIL
IS A SOPHISTICATED LATE-NIGHT REVIVER.

30 ml/1 fl oz. Gordon's Sloe Gin, or similar sloe gin

5 fresh blackberries

$\frac{1}{2}$ teaspoon good-quality balsamic vinegar

$\frac{1}{2}$ teaspoon Chambord (optional)

well-chilled Prosecco, to top up

ice cubes

MAKES 1

Put the blackberries in a cocktail shaker with
the balsamic vinegar and crush to release all their
juice. Add the sloe gin, Chambord (if using) and
a handful of ice cubes and shake well. Strain
into a flute or ice-filled rocks glass, as preferred,
and slowly top up with Prosecco.
Serve immediately.

Petal Pink

THIS IS A PRETTY AND ELEGANT COCKTAIL WITH A DELICATE FLORAL
PERFUME THANKS TO THE INCLUSION OF A PINK GIN INFUSED
WITH ROSE PETALS AND HIBISCUS.

30 ml/1 fl oz. Eden Mill Love Gin,
or similar rose-forward, floral pink gin

1 large fresh strawberry, hulled

25 ml/^{3}/$_4$ fl oz. simple sugar syrup

2 teaspoons freshly squeezed lemon juice

about 75 ml/2^1/$_2$ fl oz. well-chilled
sparkling pale rosé wine

edible rose petal, to garnish

ice cubes

SERVES 1

Put the strawberry and sugar syrup in a cocktail shaker and lightly
crush. Add the gin and lemon juice and a handful of ice cubes and
shake. Strain into an ice-filled rocks glass and slowly top up with the
sparkling wine. Garnish with a rose petal and serve immediately.

Cherry 75

THIS GIN-BASED DELIGHT IS SIMILAR TO A FRENCH 75 IN STYLE, WITH
THE CHERRY-FLAVOURED PINK GIN GIVING IT A LITTLE CANDIED WARMTH.

60 ml/2 fl oz. J.J. Whitley Pink Cherry Gin,
or similar cherry-flavoured pink gin

15 ml/^{1}/$_2$ fl oz. freshly squeezed lemon juice

15 ml/^{1}/$_2$ fl oz. simple sugar syrup

200 ml/7 fl oz. well-chilled sparkling
fruity rosé wine

edible flowers or fresh cherries,
to garnish (optional)

ice cubes

SERVES 2

Add the gin, lemon juice, sugar syrup and a handful of ice cubes
to a cocktail shaker and shake for a few seconds. Strain the mixture
into coupes, slowly top up with the chilled sparkling rosé and
garnish with edible flowers or a cherry. Serve immediately.

COOLERS

Spicy Berry Cooler

HERE IS A SIMPLE PUNCH THAT REQUIRES MINIMUM EFFORT, BUT
TASTES DELICIOUS NONETHELESS. IT NEEDS TO SIT IN THE FRIDGE
OVERNIGHT TO ALLOW THE BERRIES TO MACERATE IN THE WINE
AND GIN. THE HINT OF SPICE FROM THE SPARKLING
GINGER ALE ADDS A TOUCH OF SPICE.

150 ml/5 fl oz. Rives Pink Gin,
or similar strawberry-forward, fruity pink gin

1 x 750-ml/25-fl oz. bottle fruity and sweet rosé wine

100 g/1 cup fresh strawberries, hulled and sliced

100 g/³/₄ cup fresh raspberries

50 g/¹/₄ cup white caster/superfine sugar

1 litre/4 cups well-chilled sparkling ginger ale

1 orange, thinly sliced, to serve

ice cubes

SERVES 6–8

Pour the wine and gin into a large jug/pitcher and add the
strawberries, raspberries and sugar. Cover and marinate
overnight in the fridge. When ready to serve, pour the ginger
ale into the jug/pitcher and stir. Add ice cubes and pour into
ice cube-filled tumblers. Add a few berries to each serving
and garnish with orange slices. Serve immediately.

The Pink & the Green

A FRAGRANT AND DELICATE SUMMER CUP THAT PERFECTLY
SHOWCASES A PALE PINK GIN DISTILLED FROM PROVENÇAL
GRAPES AND INFUSED WITH HERBS AND BOTANICALS.

75 ml/2$\frac{1}{2}$ fl oz. Terres de Mistral Provence Gin,
or similar herbal, dry pale pink gin

1 x 750-ml/25-fl oz. bottle well-chilled pale Provençal rosé wine

250 ml/1 cup elderflower cordial

125 ml/$\frac{1}{2}$ cup freshly squeezed lemon juice

30 ml/1 fl oz. rosewater

1–1$\frac{1}{2}$ litres/4–6 cups well-chilled tonic water
(Fever Tree Elderflower works well here, if available)

cucumber slices and lemon wheels, to serve

edible rose petals, to garnish (optional)

ice cubes

SERVES 6–8

Pour the gin, rosé wine, elderflower cordial,
lemon juice and rosewater into a large punch bowl.
Add plenty of ice cubes to chill, then add tonic to taste.
Follow with the cucumber and lemon slices and stir.
Scatter over the rose petals just before serving, if using.
Ladle into ice cube-filled white wine glasses, adding
a little of the fruit and edible rose petals
to each glass (if using). Serve immediately.

Spanish Strawberry

IN VALENCIA, THE STRAWBERRY *GIN TONICA* IS NOT MADE BY
PAIRING THE GIN WITH TONIC WATER, BUT LEMON FANTA!

50 ml/1⅔ fl oz. Poetic License Strawberry
& Cream Picnic Gin,
or similar strawberry-forward, fruity gin

120 ml/4 fl oz. Lemon Fanta (or bitter
lemon for a tarter drink)

fresh strawberries, hulled and
quartered, to serve

lemon zests, to garnish

ice cubes

SERVES 1

Fill a large balloon glass with ice cubes. Pour in the gin and stir
to chill. Top up with the Lemon Fanta and serve immediately
with strawberries and lemon zests.

Hibiscus Gin & Tonic

HERE'S A DELICIOUSLY TROPICAL TAKE ON A CLASSIC.

30 ml/1 fl oz. Pinckney Bend Hibiscus Gin,
or similar floral-forward pink gin

15 ml/1 tablespoon hibiscus syrup,
such as Monin

100 ml/3⅓ fl oz. well-chilled tonic water

1 edible fresh hibiscus flower,
to garnish (optional)

ice cubes

SERVES 1

Put the hibiscus syrup in a balloon glass,
add the gin, top up with tonic, add ice
cubes and stir. Garnish with a flower
and serve immediately.

Raspberry Rickey

A LUSH BERRY PINK GIN MADE WITH FRESH SCOTTISH
RASPBERRIES WORKS PERFECTLY IN THIS FRUITY VERSION
OF A CLASSIC RICKEY COCKTAIL. THE PERFECT DRINK
TO SIP ON A BALMY SUMMER EVENING.

30 ml/1 fl oz. Square Peg Pink Gin,
or similar raspberry-forward, fruity pink gin

4 fresh raspberries

20 ml/^{2}/$_3$ fl oz. freshly squeezed lime juice

a dash of Chambord

well-chilled soda water, to top up

a lime slice, to garnish

ice cubes

SERVES 1

Crush the raspberries in the bottom of a highball
glass. Fill with ice cubes, add the remaining
ingredients and stir gently. Garnish with a lime
slice and serve with a paper straw.

La Passeggiata

THE *PASSEGGIATA* IS AN EXCELLENT ITALIAN TRADITION OF
TAKING AN EVENING STROLL ALONG A SCENIC BOULEVARD,
DRESSED UP TO THE NINES. WHY NOT GIVE IT A TRY,
FUELLED BY ONE OF THESE TANGY SPRITZES?

20 ml/^{3}/$_4$ fl oz. Whitley Neill Pink Grapefruit Gin,
or similar grapefruit-forward, citrusy gin

75 ml/2^1/$_2$ fl oz. well-chilled pink grapefruit juice

20 ml/^{3}/$_4$ fl oz. Aperol

well-chilled Prosecco, to top up

a pink grapefruit wedge, to garnish

ice cubes

SERVES 1

Half-fill a collins glass with ice cubes. Add the gin, pink
grapefruit juice and Aperol and stir well. Add a thin
wedge of pink grapefruit, slowly top up with Prosecco
and stir very briefly. Serve immediately.

Iced G & Tea

TEA, GIN AND PROSECCO: ALL YOUR FAVOURITE REFRESHMENTS IN ONE GLASS! HEAVEN. NEXT TIME YOU FANCY A LONG ISLAND ICED TEA, THINK AGAIN, AND TRY THIS FAR MORE ELEGANT COCKTAIL INSTEAD.

30 ml/1 fl oz. Gin Lane 1751 Victoria Pink Gin, or similar traditional-style pink gin

1 Earl Grey tea bag

1 tablespoon caster/superfine sugar

1 teaspoon freshly squeezed lemon juice

a dash of elderflower cordial

well-chilled Prosecco, to top up

lemon slices, to garnish

ice cubes

SERVES 1

Put the tea bag and sugar in a small heatproof jug/pitcher and pouring over 75 ml/2^1/2 fl oz. boiling water, then leave for 5 minutes. Remove the tea bag and leave to cool to room temperature. Pour the cooled Earl Grey infusion into a highball glass and add the gin, lemon juice and elderflower cordial. Half-fill with ice cubes and stir well. Slowly top up with Prosecco and garnish with a couple of lemon slices.

Strawberry Mule

BREAK THE ICE WITH THIS FRUITIER VERSION OF
THE CLASSIC MOSCOW MULE. THIS RECIPE IS MADE WITH
A GIN LIQUEUR, WHICH, ALTHOUGH STILL MADE WITH
DISTILLED GIN, IS SWEETER AND HAS A LOWER ALCOHOL
CONTENT, SO IS A GREAT CHOICE FOR LONG SUMMER
DRINKS LIKE THE MULE.

60 ml/2 fl oz. Jawbox Rhubarb and Ginger Gin Liqueur,
or similar

2 thin slices of fresh ginger

3 fresh strawberries, hulled and sliced,
plus extra (unhulled) to garnish

well-chilled sparkling ginger ale, to top up

a lime zest, to garnish

ice cubes

SERVES 1

Put the ginger and strawberries together in a
cocktail shaker and crush with a wooden muddler.
Add the gin liqueur and replace the lid. Shake,
then strain into a highball glass filled with ice.
Top up with sparkling ginger ale, stir gently
and garnish with a strawberry and lime zest.
Serve immediately with a paper straw.

Mermaid's Kiss

MAKE A SPLASH AND SERVE THIS FRAGRANT AND FUN
SUMMER COCKTAIL AT YOUR NEXT POOL PARTY.

60 ml/2 fl oz. Mermaid Pink Gin, or similar
strawberry-forward, fruity pink gin

30 ml/1 fl oz. hibiscus syrup, such as Monin

10 ml/2 teaspoons freshly squeezed lemon juice

well-chilled clear sparkling lemonade, to top up

ice cubes

SERVES 1

Half-fill a tumbler with ice cubes. Add the gin, hibiscus
syrup and lemon juice. Top up with chilled lemonade
and stir gently before serving immediately
with paper straws.

Berry Collins

THIS ZESTY, REFRESHING LONG DRINK IS A TWIST ON THE
ORIGINAL GIN COCKTAIL AND GUARANTEED TO CHILL
OUT YOUR SUMMER GUESTS

500 ml/2 cups Redcastle Raspberry & Pomegranate Gin Liqueur,
or similar pomegranate-flavoured gin liqueur

freshly squeezed juice of 6 lemons

125 ml/4 1/4 fl oz. fresh raspberry or pomegranate cocktail purée
(see page 9)

100 ml/3 1/3 fl oz. simple sugar syrup

well-chilled soda water, to top up

lemon slices, to serve

ice cubes

SERVES 10

Add the gin liqueur, lemon juice, raspberry or
pomegranate purée and sugar syrup to a large jug/
pitcher or punch bowl filled with ice cubes and stir
gently to mix. Top up slowly with chilled soda water
and stir again. Pour into tall ice-filled glasses,
add a lemon slice and serve immediately.

Summer Punch

DELICIOUSLY FRESH AND FRUITY, THIS GIN-BASED SUMMER PUNCH IS THE PERFECT DRINK TO SERVE AT GARDEN PARTIES AND PICNICS.

300 ml/2¼ cups Echo Falls Summer Berries Pink Gin, or similar red berry-forward, fruity pink gin

250 g/2 cups mixed fresh berries, plus extra to garnish (strawberries, raspberries and blueberries)

1 small orange, sliced

2 litres/8 cups unsweetened cranberry juice

1 small cucumber, peeled, deseeded and sliced

well-chilled clear sparkling lemonade, to top up

ice cubes

SERVES 12

Put the berries, orange slices, gin and cranberry juice in a large jug/pitcher or punch bowl and chill in the fridge for 1 hour. When ready to serve, add the cucumber and ice cubes and and top up with the lemonade. Pour or ladle into punch glasses or tumblers and garnish each one with fresh berries skewered onto a toothpick/cocktail stick.

Watermelon Gin & Lime Cooler

THIS JUICY WATERMELON AND GIN COOLER IS
GUARANTEED TO KEEP YOU COOL EVEN ON
THE HOTTEST OF DAYS.

500 ml/2 cups Verano Spanish Watermelon Gin,
Two Birds Watermelon Gin, or similar watermelon-flavoured gin

500 g/8 cups watermelon chunks, with seeds removed

125 ml/^{1}/$_2$ cup freshly squeezed lime juice

60 ml/^{1}/$_4$ cup simple sugar syrup

250 ml/1 cup well-chilled Cava

crushed ice

SERVES 14

Whizz up the watermelon pieces in a blender,
then pass through a very fine sieve/strainer set over
a large jug/pitcher. Discard any bits of seeds
left in the sieve-strainer.

Stir in the gin, lime juice, sugar syrup and cava.
Half-fill high ball glasses with crushed ice and pour
in the cocktail to fill. Serve immediately.

Index

Recipe credits

Photography credits